First Steps in Using Rational Emotive Behaviour Therapy in Coaching

By the same author
and published by Rationality Publications

*When Time Is at a Premium: Cognitive-Behavioural Approaches to
Single-Session Therapy and Very Brief Coaching* (2016)
*Attitudes in Rational Emotive Behaviour Therapy (REBT):
Components, Characteristics and Adversity-Related
Consequences* (2016)
Windy Dryden Live! (2021)
Windy Dryden Collected! (2022)
*The REBT Pocket Companion for Clients, 2nd Edition
(with Walter J. Matweychuk)* (2022)
The Little Book of Therapeutic Rationality (2022)
*Thought for the Day: A Flexible Approach to
Mental Health* (2022)
*Seizing Moments and Being Useful: The Development of a Single-
Session Therapist* (2025)
WWW: The Collected Wonderful Words of Windy (2025)

'Seven Principles' Series

Seven Principles of Good Mental Health (2021)
Seven Principles of Rational Emotive Behaviour Therapy (2021)
Seven Principles of Single-Session Therapy (2021)
Seven Principles of Doing Live Therapy Demonstrations (2021)

'First Steps' Series

*First Steps in Rational Emotive Behaviour Therapy: A Guide to
Practising REBT in Peer Counselling, 2nd Edition* (2025)
First Steps in Rational Emotive Behaviour Therapy for Clients (2025)
*First Steps in Using Rational Emotive Behaviour Therapy in
Coaching* (2025)
First Steps in Single-Session Therapy (2025)

First Steps in Using Rational Emotive Behaviour Therapy in Coaching

Second Edition

Windy Dryden

Rationality Publications

Rationality Publications
136 Montagu Mansions, London W1U 6LQ

www.rationalitypublications.com
info@rationalitypublications.com

Second edition published by Rationality Publications
Copyright (c) 2025 Windy Dryden

First edition published by the Albert Ellis Institute in 2011

ISBN: 978-1-914938-44-3

Contents

Introduction

Your basic goal as a coach is to help your coachee identify, pursue and ultimately achieve their personal objectives,[1] not help them with their emotional problems per se. That is the role of the psychotherapist or counsellor. You should only deal with your coachee's emotional problem when it serves as a specific obstacle to them pursuing their personal objectives because she have become stuck in an unhealthy way of responding to adversity. If your coachee has many such problems, refer them to a psychotherapist or counsellor so they can subsequently engage in coaching productively. However, if your coachee can respond productively to this unhealthy emotion using their own resources, then let them do so and don't intervene. If you make such an intervention, you might indicate to your coachee that they are not capable of dealing with such obstacles on their own when they have such capability.

There are a number of approaches to helping coachees with their emotional problems in coaching and it is important that you understand something of the one I will be discussing in this book. This is known as Rational Emotive Behaviour Therapy (REBT). REBT is based on an old idea attributed to Epictetus, a Roman philosopher, who said that 'Men are disturbed not by things, but by their views of things.' In REBT, we have modified this to say that 'People are disturbed not by things, but by the rigid and extreme attitudes that they hold towards things.' Once they have disturbed themselves they then try to get rid of their disturbed

---

[1] In this book, by personal objectives I mean objectives that, if realised, would indicate that your coachee is getting the most from themself in one or more important domains of their life.

feelings in ways that ultimately serve to maintain their problems. I begin the book by presenting an overview of REBT's *Situational ABC* framework that you will use while helping your coachee deal with their emotional problems during coaching. When you use REBT in coaching, you will help your coachees to identify, examine and change the rigid and extreme attitudes that, from an REBT perspective, underpin their emotional problems and to develop alternative flexible and non-extreme attitudes. You will also help them examine the ways in which they have tried to help themselves that haven't worked and encourage them to develop and practice more effective, longer-lasting strategies. In helping your coachees to deal with their emotional problems, you will teach them a framework which helps them to break down their problems into their constituent parts. You will also teach them a variety of methods for examining and changing their rigid and extreme attitudes and a variety of methods to help them consolidate and strengthen their alternative flexible and non-extreme attitudes.

This step-by-step guide shows you how to deal with your coachee's emotional problem when it prevents them from working toward their personal objectives using the theory and practice of REBT adapted to a coaching setting.

Windy Dryden
London, Eastbourne, December 2024

REBT's *Situational ABC* Framework

The practice of Rational Emotive Behaviour Therapy is based on an understanding of people's disturbed and healthy responses to life's adversities. This is known as the *Situational ABC* framework and is particularly relevant to the general practice of REBT, where the therapist is encouraged to work with a specific example of the coachee's[2] nominated[3] problem.

As noted above, the *Situational ABC* framework provides an explanation for both your coachee's disturbed response (*C*) to an adversity (*A*) in a specific *Situation* and their potential healthy response (*C*) to the same adversity (*A*). What determines this response is the basic attitude (*B*) that your client holds towards the adversity: rigid/extreme in the case of a disturbed response to the adversity; flexible/non-extreme in the case of a healthy response to the same adversity. This is shown in Table 1 (next page).[4]

I will use this framework in outlining the steps you need to take while dealing with your coachee's emotional problems in coaching.

---

[2] Throughout this book, I will refer to the person you are helping as a 'coachee'.

[3] In this book, a coachee's nominated problem refers to the problem that the person nominates to address with their coach. It is the problem that interferes with them pursuing their coaching objectives.

[4] I will expand on each element of this framework at the appropriate place in the book.

Table 1 REBT's *Situational ABC* Framework
explaining psychological disturbance and health

Situation
(Where the specific example of your coachee's nominated problem took place)

Adversity (*A*)
(The aspect of the *Situation* to which your coachee responded in a disturbed way and to which they could respond healthily)

Rigid/Extreme Attitude (*B*)	Flexible/Non-Extreme Attitude (*B*)
• Rigid Attitude ↓	• Flexible Attitude ↓
• Awfulising Attitude	• Non-Awfulising Attitude
• Unbearability Attitude	• Bearability Attitude
• Devaluation Attitude	• Unconditional Acceptance Attitude
Unhealthy Negative Emotion, Unconstructive Behaviour and Highly Distorted Negative Thinking (*C*)	Healthy Negative Emotion, Constructive Behaviour and Realistic and Balanced Thinking (*C*)

STEP 1

Determine Whether Your Coachee Has an Emotional Problem. If So, Are They Stuck or Are They Still Able to Pursue Their Personal Objectives?

1.1   Does your coachee have an emotional problem?

The nine main unhealthy emotions that coachees experience when faced with life's adversities are:

- anxiety
- depression
- shame
- guilt
- hurt
- unhealthy regret
- unhealthy anger
- unhealthy jealousy
- unhealthy envy

These are known as unhealthy negative emotions (UNEs) in REBT and it is important that you assess whether or not your coachee has an emotional problem. You do this by answering the following questions:

1.2   Is your coachee stuck?

Just because your coachee experiences a UNE about an adversity doesn't justify you helping them with it. Many people experience UNEs temporarily without them becoming emotional problems and can resolve them on their own. It's only when your coachee gets bogged down and can't move on in pursuing their personal objectives either by themself or with others' help that they require your intervention. So, intervene:

1.2.1   If there's been no change in your coachee's disturbed feelings despite extended attempts at:
- self-help
- seeking informal help from others;

1.2.2   If they have no plans to deal with this emotional problem in the future and it is likely to continue

1.3   Is your coachee's emotional problem preventing them from pursuing their personal objectives?

Your coachee's emotional problem will not necessarily prevent them from pursuing the personal objectives they set with you earlier in the coaching process. If they are stuck, it's unlikely but not impossible that they will have the mental space to detach from the problem and pursue their personal objectives (coaching goals). If they can compartmentalise their emotional problem despite being stuck, and can keep working toward their personal objectives, you have three ways forward:

1.3.1 **Keep helping your coachee to work toward their personal objectives without helping them deal with their emotional problem**

Leave them to decide if and how they want to tackle it.

1.3.2 **Keep helping your coachee their work toward their personal objectives and offer to help them get unstuck with respect to the emotional problem**

In doing so, you recognise that you are moving into a counselling role with them and therefore your coaching contract with them may need to be renegotiated.

1.3.3 **Keep helping your coachee work toward their personal objectives and refer them to a counsellor who will help them with their emotional problem**

Which of these options you choose depends on how you construe your coaching role and on the views of your coachee. Some coaches choose not to take a counselling role and will therefore not take the option outlined in 1.3.2. Others are happy to move from coaching to counselling and back again. Any movement from coaching to counselling needs careful exploration with your coachee and explicit agreement with them. Finally, it is best to avoid switching from coaching to counselling with coachees who have particular difficulties handling *Situations* where roles are ambiguous.

STEP 2

Elicit Your Coachee's Explicit Agreement to Address Their Emotional Problem for Change and Establish a Contingency Plan if You Fail to Help Them

Developing a good working alliance between you and your coachee is vital to effective coaching. Such an alliance depends on you both (a) having a good bond, (b) having a shared view of the coaching process, (c) agreeing on their personal objectives and (d) agreeing on what you are both going to do to help them achieve their objectives (Dryden, 2017).

Consider what you both will do if your attempts to help your coachee with their emotional problem are not successful. Making a contingency plan at this stage is good ethical practice.

2.1 Renegotiate your contract with your coachee from a coaching contract to a counselling contract and then refer them to a different coach

This means you will help them with this problem more intensively and with any other emotional problems they may have and refer them to another coach when they are ready to resume their pursuit of their personal objectives.

2.2 Renegotiate your contract with your coachee from a coaching contract to a counselling contract and then revert to a coaching contract when the coachee is ready to resume coaching

This means you will help them with this problem more intensively and with any other emotional problems they may have. When they are ready to resume their pursuit of their personal objectives, revert back to a coaching contract.

2.3 Refer your coachee to a counsellor who will work with them on this emotional problem until they are ready to resume their coaching work with you

Some coaches who are also trained counsellors will agree a contract with their coachees which includes both counselling and coaching work. This means that there is no need to effect a referral to another counsellor/coach since that person will do both types of work with their clients/coachees.

2.4 If you are a trained coach and counsellor, negotiate a contract that covers both areas of work

Rather than go backwards and forwards, if you are a trained coach and a trained counsellor, you can negotiate a contract with your coachee covering both work areas. This means that the two of you can move seamlessly between coaching and counselling. However, as most coaches are not trained counsellors, I will not take this tack in this book.

STEP 3

Formulate the Problem Serving as an Obstacle to Pursuing Your Coachee's Personal Objectives

When you agree to work with your coachee on the problem which is proving to be an obstacle to them working towards their personal objectives, you need to make clear what framework you will be using with them.

3.1 Formulate your coachee's emotional problem using key elements of REBT's *Situational ABC* framework

When you focus on an emotional obstacle to the pursuit of your coachee's personal objectives in the context of coaching, you will only deal with a single specific problem. Otherwise, you will be involved in counselling, not coaching. Obtain a clear statement of this problem by formulating your coachee's emotional problem using REBT's *Situational ABC* framework.

Situation – Help your coachee identify the *Situation* in which they experience their problem.

A – The aspect of the *Situation* she was most disturbed about. (You will do this more explicitly in Step 8.)

C **(emotional)** – Help them identify **one** of the following major unhealthy negative emotions (UNEs) they are experiencing: anxiety, depression, guilt, shame, hurt, unhealthy regret, unhealthy anger, unhealthy jealousy, unhealthy envy.

C **(behavioural)** – Help them identify the dysfunctional behaviour they demonstrated in this *Situation*, e.g. an overt action or action tendency.

C **(thinking)** – Help them identify the thinking she engaged in once their UNE emerged. This thinking is highly distorted and skewed to the negative.

Effect on coaching goals – Help them specify the effect this emotional problem has on their overall personal objectives (coaching goals).

STEP 4

Set a Goal with Respect to the Formulated Problem

After you have helped your coachee to formulate their problem, it is important that you have them see where they want to go with respect to this problem so that you are moving in the same direction.

4.1 Set your coachee's goal with respect to their formulated problem using the same key elements of the *Situational ABC* framework

Helping your coachee set a goal regarding their formulated problem will give your work on their emotional problem a sense of direction, help them see that change is possible, engender a sense of hope, and increase their motivation to engage in the REBT process. Use the following points to help them set a goal regarding their formulated emotional problem.

Situation – This will be the same as your coachee specified in their formulated problem.

A – This will again be the same as your coachee specified in their formulated problem. You will do this more explicitly in Step 8.

C **(emotional goal)** – Help them identify the healthy alternative to the major UNE she experienced. This is known as a healthy negative emotion (HNE). This emotional goal should be negative because it is about adversity, but it should also be healthy as it will help them deal effectively with the adversity if it can be changed or adjust constructively to it if it can't. This will be: concern (UNE: anxiety), sadness (UNE: depression), remorse (UNE: guilt), disappointment (UNE: shame), sorrow (UNE: hurt), healthy regret (UNE: unhealthy regret), healthy anger (UNE: unhealthy anger), healthy jealousy (UNE: unhealthy jealousy); healthy envy (UNE: unhealthy envy).

C **(behavioural goal)** – Help them identify the functional alternative to the unconstructive behaviour they demonstrated in their formulated problem. Again, this might be an overt action or an action tendency.

C **(thinking goal)** – If relevant, help them identify the realistic alternative to the highly negatively distorted thinking they engaged in.

Effect on coaching goals – Help them specify the effect these goals with respect to their emotional problem are likely to have on their overall personal objectives (coaching goals).

STEP 5

Assess the Presence of a Meta-Emotional Problem and Decide with the Coachee if This Is to Become Their Nominated Problem

5.1 Assess the existence of a meta-emotional problem

When your coachee has an emotional problem, they may focus on this problem and disturb themself about it. Thus, you should determine the possible existence of a meta-emotional problem (an emotional problem about an emotional or behavioural problem). Ask them, e.g.

- *How do you feel about … [state their original emotional/behavioural problem]?*

5.2 What to do if your coachee has a meta-emotional problem

If your coachee has a meta-emotional problem, decide with them if you need to deal with this before you both focus on their original problem. Suggest to them that you both focus on their original emotional/behavioural problem unless:

- They want to work on their meta-emotional problem first
- Their meta-emotional problem interferes with them focusing on their original emotional/behavioural problem in the session;
- Their meta-emotional problem interferes with them working on their original emotional/behavioural problem in their life.

Both of you should agree on which problem (the original or their meta-emotional problem) to work on first. If you address their original problem and help them with this effectively, you may not need to help them with their meta-emotional problem if they can resume work on their personal objective (coaching goal) without doing so.

STEP 6

Ask for a Concrete Example of the Coachee's Formulated Problem

At this point in the process, it is important that you and your coachee work as specifically as possible. Resist the temptation to move from the specific to the general and discourage your coachee from doing the same.

6.1 Help your coachee select a concrete example of their formulated problem

Working with a concrete example will provide both you and your coachee with specific information about your coachee's A and C to help you identify a specific rigid/extreme attitude at B. If their problem is specific enough anyway, you may skip this step. If not, ask them:

> • *Can you give me a concrete example of this problem?*

A concrete example occurs in a specific *Situation* at a specific time with a specific person or persons being present and could be real or imagined. If your coachee finds it difficult to select such an example, you can suggest they pick an example which is fresh in their mind, which might be:

- recent
- vivid
- typical
- future

It may seem strange to talk about a future example of your coachee's problem, but it is not really so strange. They may imagine a future scenario and disturb themself about it because they bring a disturbance-creating rigid/extreme attitude to that future event.

STEP 7

Identify *C*

In this circumstance, *C* represents your coachee's disturbed emotional, behavioural and thinking responses to an adversity at *A* mediated as these are by the person's rigid/extreme attitude at *B*. This is why *C* stands for consequences. They are consequences of the person's basic attitudes.

7.1 Start with the emotional *C*

Sometimes, your coachee may not have specified their unhealthy negative emotion in formulating their problem, and it is only when they discuss a specific example of the problem that the relevant UNE becomes clear. As mentioned above, *C*, the consequences of the rigid/extreme attitude that they hold towards *A*, can be emotional, behavioural and cognitive. You should assess your coachee's major UNE in the selected example.

Starting with *C*, particularly their major UNE, will help you identify their *A* by indicating the likely theme of *A* (see Appendix 1). For example, if your coachee says that they feel anxious, the theme of 'threat' may be present in their *A*. Ask them to identify how they felt in the *Situation*. Help them select one UNE and, if they felt several, help them identify the main one.

Ask:

- ***How did you feel when ...... (state the Situation) ...?***

Your coachee should state that their emotional C is negative and unhealthy. However, you may encounter a number of problematic scenarios.

7.2   When your coachee's emotional C is vague

Your coachee may say they feel bad or upset. Such expressions are unclear: you still don't know their negative emotional C, nor if it is unhealthy or healthy. If so, help them be more specific about their feelings.

7.3   You are not sure if your coachee's negative C is healthy or unhealthy

If you are not sure whether your coachee's stated emotion is a UNE or an HNE (healthy negative emotion), consult Appendix 1. Here, you will see that apart from the different names given to UNE/HNE pairs, each emotion within a pairing (e.g. anxiety and concern) is associated with different behaviours (i.e. overt actions and action tendencies) and subsequent thinking. You may thus deduce your coachee's emotion by discovering how they acted in the *Situation* under assessment and/or how she thought after their feelings had 'kicked in'.

7.4   When your coachee's stated emotional *C* is really an inference

An inference is an interpretation your coachee made about their *Situation*, relating to their emotional response, but which went beyond the data at hand. This 'inference as emotion' often turns out to be your coachee's *A*, e.g.

- *I felt rejected*
- *I felt wronged*

Neither of these represent your coachee's emotional *C* but are inferences. When your coachee says they 'felt wronged', for example, they mean that the person in the example of their emotional problem acted in a way that transgressed one of their rules. They may well have experienced an emotion about 'being wronged', which is a UNE (i.e. negative and unhealthy), but you should help them be explicit about this. Thus, when your coachee offers you an inference instead of an emotion in response to your enquiry about their emotional *C*, treat their response as an inference and ask them how they felt *about* it. When your coachee gives you an inference instead of an emotion, remember to use the inference to identify the emotional *C*; resist the temptation to question the inference.

7.5   Ask for behavioural and/or thinking *Cs* and infer the emotional

If your coachee continues to struggle to give you an emotional *C*, you can temporarily bypass this and infer the emotion from their behaviour (overt action and action tendency) or their subsequent thinking. Before doing so, familiarise yourself with Appendix 1. Here is a suggested process.

- Ask them to imagine they are in the *Situation* they selected in which they experienced their emotional problem.
- Assess how they acted in this *Situation* or what they felt like doing but didn't do.
- If necessary, ask them what thoughts they had after their yet-to-be-identified feelings had 'kicked in'.
- Form a hypothesis concerning their emotional *C*, given their behavioural *C* and/or thinking *C*.
- Ask them to consider and respond to this hypothesis.

STEP 8

Identify *A*

I distinguish between *A* (the adversity in the *Situation* about which your coachee was most disturbed) and the *Situation* in which they were disturbed. *A* is usually an inference, while the *Situation* is descriptive.

The best way I have found to assess *A* is using *Windy's Magic Question* (WMQ). Here is how to use this method. There are two questions you can ask:

Windy's Magic Question (WMQ)

- Step 1. Have the coachee focus on their disturbed *C* (*e.g. anxiety*)

- Step 2: Encourage the coachee to focus on the *Situation* in which *C* occurred (e.g. *Learning that their line manager wants to see them*)

- Step 3: Ask the coachee: Which ingredient could I give you to eliminate or significantly reduce *C* (here, *anxiety*)? (In this case, the coachee said: *My line manager not criticising my work*). Take care that the coachee does not change the *Situation* (i.e. they do not say: My line manager does not want to see me)

- Step 4: The opposite is probably *A* (e.g. *my line manager criticising my work*), but check. Ask: *So, when you were waiting to see your line manager, were you most anxious about her criticising your work?* If not, ask the question listed in Step 3 and then the question listed above until the coachee confirms what they were most anxious about in the described *Situation*

You may find Table 2 (next page) useful in helping your coachee to identify their *A*. It lists the themes of the adversity at *A* associated with the nine unhealthy negative emotions cited above.

Once you have identified your coachee's *A*, it is very important that you resist any temptation to question it, even if it is obviously distorted. Encourage your coachee to assume that their *A* is true, albeit temporarily. This will let you identify their rigid and extreme attitudes at *B* later.

Let's assume for the moment that …….. (state *A*) …. happened. It may not have happened, but let's assume, temporarily, that it did.

For example:

- *Let's assume for the moment that your line manager does criticise your work. This may not happen, but let's assume, temporarily, that it does.*

Table 2 Adversities at A related to unhealthy negative emotions at C^5

Adversity at A	Unhealthy Negative Emotion at C
• Threat	• Anxiety
• Loss • Failure • Undeserved plight (to self/others)	• Depression
• Breaking your moral code • Failing to live up to your moral code • Hurting/harming someone	• Guilt
• Something highly negative has been revealed about you (or about a group with whom you identify) by you or by others • Falling very short of your ideal • Others look down on or shun you (or a group with whom you identify)	• Shame
• Someone betrays you or lets you down, and you think you do not deserve such treatment • Another is not as invested in your relationship with them as you are	• Hurt
• You or another transgresses your personal rule • Another threatens your self-esteem • Frustration	• Unhealthy Anger
• Wishing you had not taken a course of action that you took • Wishing that you had taken a course of action that you didn't take	• Unhealthy Regret
• Threat to a valued relationship • Uncertainty related to that threat	• Unhealthy Jealousy
• Others have what you value and lack	• Unhealthy Envy

---

[5] Please note that the nine healthy negative emotions listed in Table 2 also relate to the same adversities. Thus, the threat is the adversity that features in both anxiety and concern.

STEP 9

Identify the Coachee's Rigid and Extreme Attitudes and Help Them to See the Flexible and Non-Extreme Alternatives to these Attitudes at *B*

At this point, you need to help your coachee understand that their disturbed reactions at *C* are determined neither by the *Situation* nor by their inference at *A* but largely by their rigid and extreme attitudes at *B*. There are several methods of doing this. The one that I think is the most efficient is what I call *Windy's Review Assessment Procedure* (WRAP). It is used to assess the coachee's specific rigid and extreme attitudes in the example selected by the coachee, but it also helps the coachee see what their flexible and non-extreme attitudes are that will form the attitude-based solution to their problem. In using this method, I suggest that you identify the coachee's rigid attitude and the one extreme attitude that best accounts for their unhealthy negative emotion.

Windy's Review Assessment Procedure (WRAP)

1. Begin by saying: *Let's review what we know and what we don't know so far.*

2. Then, say: *We know three things.*

First, we know that you were anxious (C).

Second, we know that you were anxious about your line manager line manager criticising your work (A).

Third, and this is an educated guess on my part, we know that it is important to you that your line manager does not criticise your work. Am I correct?

Assuming that the coachee confirms your hunch, note that what you have done is to identify the part of the attitude that is common to both the coachee's rigid attitude and alternative flexible attitude, as we will see.

3. Continue by saying: *Let's review what we don't know. This is where I need your help. We don't know which of two attitudes your anxiety was based on. So, when you were anxious about your line manager criticising your work, was your anxiety based on Attitude 1: It is important to me that my line manager does not criticise my work and therefore, they must not do so (Rigid attitude) or Attitude 2: It is important to me that my line manager does not criticise my work, but that does not mean that they must not do so (Flexible attitude)?*

4. If necessary, help the coachee to understand that their *anxiety* was based on their rigid attitude if they are unsure.

5. Once the coachee is clear that their *anxiety* was based on their rigid attitude, make and emphasise the rigid attitude-disturbed *C* connection. Then, ask:

Let's suppose instead that you had a strong conviction in attitude 2. How would you feel about your line manager criticising your work if you strongly believed that while it is important to you that they do not criticise your work, it does not mean that they must not do so?

6. If necessary, help the coachee to nominate a healthy negative emotion, such as *concern*, if not immediately volunteered, and make and emphasise the flexible attitude–healthy *C* connection.

7. Ensure that the coachee clearly understands the differences between the two *B–C* connections.

8. Encourage the coachee to set *concern* as the emotional goal in this *Situation* and to see that developing conviction in their flexible attitude is the best way of achieving this goal.

Once you have identified your coachee's rigid and flexible attitudes, you can teach them the other three extreme attitudes and their non-extreme attitude alternatives (listed in Table 1 in the section entitled REBT's *Situational ABC* Framework above), and ask them to choose the one other extreme attitude that best accounted for their unhealthy negative emotion at *C* (and by implication the alternative non-extreme attitude that will help them to achieve their goal).

STEP 10

Preparing the Coachee for the Attitude Examining Process

10.1 Help the coachee to understand that the first step to change their attitudes is to examine them

You have now identified your coachee's rigid/extreme attitude and its alternative flexible/non-extreme attitude and have helped them to see the connection between the former and their unhealthy negative emotion (and/or dysfunctional behaviour) at *C* and the connection between the latter and the alternative healthy negative emotion (and/or functional behaviour) at *C*.

Your next task is to help your coachee understand that they need to examine their two sets of attitudes to determine which set they want to develop going forward.[6] The first three points review what you did at the end of Step 2.

---

[6] You will engage them in this attitude examination process in Steps 10–15.

- State the coachee's two *B–C* connections

For example:

So, you can see that if you hold a rigid attitude towards the possibility of your line manager criticising your work, you will be anxious, but if you hold a flexible attitude towards this, you will feel non-anxious concern.

- Ask the coachee for their emotional goal

For example:

Which emotion would you want to experience about this adversity?

If the coachee states the healthy negative emotion, proceed to the next step below. If they state the unhealthy negative emotion, explore why and proceed until their emotional goal is their HNE.

- Help the coachee see that they need to change their rigid/extreme attitude to achieve this goal

For example:

Given that holding a rigid attitude leads to you feel anxiety and holding a flexible attitude would lead you to feel non-anxious concern, what do you need to change to achieve your emotional goal?

Your coachee should reply 'my rigid/extreme attitude' in response. If not, explore their reasoning and proceed until they can see that changing their attitude is the best way forward.

- Explain that the first step in the attitude examination process involves you helping the coachee to examine both sets of attitudes so that they can commit to one set going forward.

For example:

The first step in this attitude change process involves me encouraging you to stand back and examine both sets of attitudes so that you can decide which set to develop going forward and the reasons for your choice. I will do this by asking you several questions about both sets of attitudes. OK? Do you have any questions before we start?

Answer any questions the coachee has and then proceed to Step 4.

10.2 How to respond if the coachee wants to change *A* and not *B*

At this point, you may find that the coachee may wish to change the adversity at *A* without changing their rigid/extreme attitude at *B* first. If this is the case, help them to see that the best time to change *A* is when they are *not* disturbed about *A* and that their disturbed feelings about *A* will interfere with their change attempts. Once they understand this and that the best way to be undisturbed about *A* is by holding a flexible/non-extreme attitude towards it, they are ready to engage in the attitude examination process.

Here is how to proceed if the coachee wants to change *A* before *B*:

Therapist: Is it best to change ..... (state *A*) when you are feeling .... (state UNE) or when you are feeling .... (state HNE)?

Coachee: When I feel .... (HNE)

[*Intervene appropriately if the coachee says UNE*]

Therapist: ....and based on what we have discussed, what do you need to change in order to feel..... (state HNE), but not ...... (state HNE) about .... (state 'A')?

Coachee: My rigid attitude

[*Intervene appropriately if the coachee gives any other answer*]

For example:

Therapist: If you decide to change how your line manager is likely to view your work, is it best to do so when you are feeling anxious or when you are feeling non-anxious concern?

Coachee:　When I feel non-anxious concern.

Therapist:　....and based on what we have discussed, what do you need to change to feel non-anxious concern about the prospect of your line manager criticising your work?

Coachee:　My rigid attitude.

Your coachee is now ready to examine their attitudes.

STEP 11

Help the Coachee to Examine Their Attitudes

11.1 The purpose of helping the coachee to examine their attitudes is for them to see that their rigid/extreme attitude is unhealthy and that their flexible/non-extreme attitude is healthy

When you help your coachee examine their rigid/extreme and flexible/non-extreme attitudes, your goal is to help them see that their rigid/extreme attitude is unhealthy (false, illogical, and yielding largely poor results) and their flexible/non-extreme attitude is healthy (true, logical and yielding largely good results). These characteristics are listed in Table 3. Helping your coachee to strengthen their conviction in their flexible/non-extreme attitude and weaken their conviction in their rigid/extreme attitude is initiated in Step 12.

11.2 Help the coachee to examine both rigid/extreme and flexible/non-extreme attitudes together

As I said above, the purpose of helping your coachee examine their attitudes is to encourage them to see that their rigid/extreme attitude is unhealthy (false, illogical and yields largely poor results) and that their alternative flexible/non-extreme attitude is healthy (true, logical and yields largely good results). This is known as intellectual insight because while the coachee understands this point, they do not yet have deep conviction in it to the extent that it influences for the better their feelings and behaviour. This 'emotional insight' will come about in ongoing counselling, but work towards its achievement is initiated in Step 5.

Table 3   Characteristics of rigid/extreme attitudes and flexible/non-extreme attitudes

Rigid/Extreme Attitudes	Flexible/Non-Extreme Attitudes
• False • Illogical • Leads to unconstructive results	• True • Logical • Leads to constructive results

To achieve such intellectual insight, your coachee must examine their rigid/extreme and flexible/non-extreme attitude. While there are several ways of doing this, in my view, the most efficient way is to help them to examine these attitudes together and I will outline this approach here.

In doing so, I suggest that you always help your coachee to examine their rigid and flexible attitudes (unless there is a good reason not to), as well as the *one* other extreme attitude that your coachee resonates with the most, together with its non-extreme attitude alternative. You do not have time to do more than this in peer counselling. The best way of doing this is to help the coachee examine these two sets of attitudes separately, as shown below.

---

1. Help the coachee examine their rigid and flexible attitudes together. Always do this unless there is a good reason not to.
2. Separately, help the coachee examine together the one extreme attitude with which they most resonate and its non-extreme attitude alternative.

  - Their unbearability and bearability attitudes
  - Their awfulising and non-awfulising attitudes
  - Their devaluation and unconditional acceptance attitudes

STEP 12

Help the Coachee to Examine a Rigid Attitude and Its Flexible Attitude Alternative

Rigid Attitude	Flexible Attitude
• *I want (don't want) X to happen, and therefore it has to be the way I want it to be*	• *I want (don't want) X to happen, but it does not have to be the way I want it to be*

I recommend that you use three main questions when helping your coachee to examine their rigid and flexible attitudes:

- The empirical question
- The logical question and
- The pragmatic question.

Then you can ask which attitude the coachee wants to strengthen and which they want to weaken and why.

First, help your coachee focus on their rigid attitude and its flexible attitude alternative. Suggest that your coachee write down both attitudes side by side (as above)[7] or write them down yourself on a whiteboard (again, as above). Then move on to the three questions. I will present them in a certain order. This order is only a guide, and other orders are fine.

12.1 The empirical question

Ask:

Which of the following attitudes is true and which is false and why?

- *The coachee's rigid attitude*
- *The coachee's flexible attitude*

According to REBT theory, the only correct answer to this question is that the flexible attitude is true and the rigid attitude is false. Help your coachee see that:

- A rigid attitude is inconsistent with reality. For such a rigid attitude to be true the conditions that the coachee is rigidly demanding to be present would already have to exist when they do not. Or, as soon as the coachee makes their rigid demand, these demanded conditions would have to exist. Both positions are patently inconsistent with reality.
- On the other hand, a flexible attitude is true since its two component parts are true. Your coachee can prove that they have a particular desire and can provide reasons why they

---

[7] You will, of course, be working with their specific rigid and flexible attitudes.

want what they want. They can also prove that they do not have to get what they desire.

If your coachee gives you any other answer then help them through discussion to see why their answer is incorrect and help her to accept the correct answer.

12.2   The logical question

Ask:

Which of the following attitudes is logical and which is illogical, and why?

- *The coachee's rigid attitude*
- *The coachee's flexible attitude*

Your coachee needs to acknowledge that their rigid attitude is illogical while their flexible attitude is logical. Help them to see that their rigid attitude is based on the same desire as their flexible attitude, but that they transform it as follows:

- **I want (don't want) X to happen, and therefore it has to be the way I want it to be**

Show the coachee that this attitude has two components. The first [I want (don't want) X to happen] is not rigid, but the second […and therefore it has to be the way I want it to be] is rigid. As such, the coachee's rigid attitude isn't logical since one cannot logically derive something rigid from something that is not rigid. Use the template in Figure 1 with your coachee to illustrate this visually, if necessary.

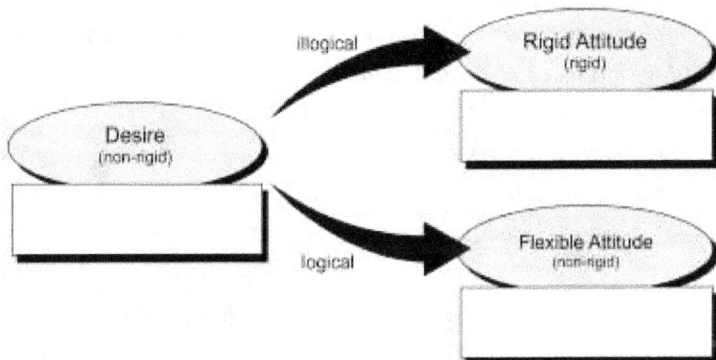

Figure 1: A rigid attitude is illogical, while a flexible attitude is logical

Your coachee's flexible attitude is as follows:

> • *I want (don't want) X to happen, but it does not have to be the way I want it to be*

The coachee's flexible attitude is logical since both parts are not rigid; thus, the second component logically follows from the first. Again, use the template in Figure 1 with your coachee to illustrate this visually, if necessary.

If your coachee gives you any other answer, then help them through discussion to see why their answer is incorrect and help them to accept the correct answer.

12.3 The pragmatic question

Ask:

Which of the following attitudes leads to largely good results and which leads to largely poor results and why?

- *The coachee's rigid attitude*
- *The coachee's flexible attitude*

You need to help your coachee acknowledge that their rigid attitude leads to largely unconstructive results, while their flexible attitude leads to more constructive ones. As you do this, use the information provided by your coachee when you discussed the two *B–C* connections (see Step10).

If your coachee thinks their rigid attitude leads to healthier consequences than their flexible attitude, help them through discussion to see why they are likely to be mistaken.

12.4 Assess the coachee's commitment to attitude change

At this point, you want to assess your coachee's commitment to change their attitude. You do this by asking the following question:

Ask:

Which attitude does the coachee want to strengthen, and which do they want to weaken and why?

- *The coachee's rigid attitude*
- *The coachee's flexible attitude*

After helping your coachee to examine their rigid and flexible attitudes, your coachee 'should' indicate that they wish to work to strengthen their conviction in their flexible attitude and weaken their conviction in their rigid attitude and be able to give coherent reasons why based on their problematic feelings and behaviour and their goals for change. If your coachee gives you any other answer, discover the reasons for this response and work with them until they fully commit to their flexible attitude.

STEP 13

Help the Coachee to Examine an Awfulising Attitude and Its Non-Awfulising Attitude Alternative

Awfulising Attitude	Non-Awfulising Attitude
• *It would be bad if X happens (or does not happen), and therefore it would be terrible*	• *It would be bad if X happens (or does not happen), but it isn't terrible*

When helping your coachee examine their awfulising and non-awfulising attitudes, use the same three questions you used to help them examine their rigid and flexible attitudes: empirical, logical, and pragmatic. Once you have done this, you can ask which attitude your coachee wants to strengthen, which they want to weaken, and why.

First, help your coachee focus on their awfulising attitude and non-awfulising attitude. Again, invite them to write them down side by side (as above)[8] or write them down yourself on a

---

[8] Again, you will be working with their specific awfulising and non-awfulising attitudes

whiteboard (again, as above). Then, move on to the three questions.

13.1   The empirical question

Ask:

Which of the following attitudes is true and which is false and why?

- *The coachee's awfulising attitude*
- *The coacher's non-awfulising attitude*

According to REBT theory, an awfulising attitude is false and a non-awfulising attitude is true.

While examining these attitudes, help your coachee see that when they are holding their awfulising attitude, they believe the following:

- Nothing could be worse;
- The event in question is worse than 100% bad
- No good could possibly come from this bad event
- They cannot transcend the event

Help your coachee see that all three convictions are inconsistent with reality and that their awfulising attitude is false. By contrast, help them to see that their non-awfulising attitude is true since this is made up of the following ideas:

- Things could always be worse;
- The event in question is less than 100% bad
- Some good could come from this bad event
- They can transcend the event

If your coachee gives you answers that is at variance with the above, then help them through discussion to see why their answer is incorrect and help them to accept the correct answer.

13.2   The logical question

Ask:

Which of the following attitudes is logical and which is illogical, and why?

- *The coachee's awfulising attitude*
- *The coachee's non-awfulising attitude*

Help your coachee see that their awfulising attitude is illogical, while their non-awfulising attitude is logical. Show them that their awfulising attitude is based on the same evaluation of badness as their non-awfulising attitude, but they transform this as follows:

> *It would be very bad if X happened (or did not happen) ….*
> *and therefore it would be terrible.*

Show your coachee that their awfulising attitude has two components. The first [It would be very bad if X happened (or did not happen)] is non-extreme, while the second (…and therefore it would be terrible) is extreme. As such, help them to see that their awfulising attitude is illogical since one cannot logically derive something extreme from something that is not extreme. Use the template in Figure 2 with your coachee to illustrate this point visually, if necessary.

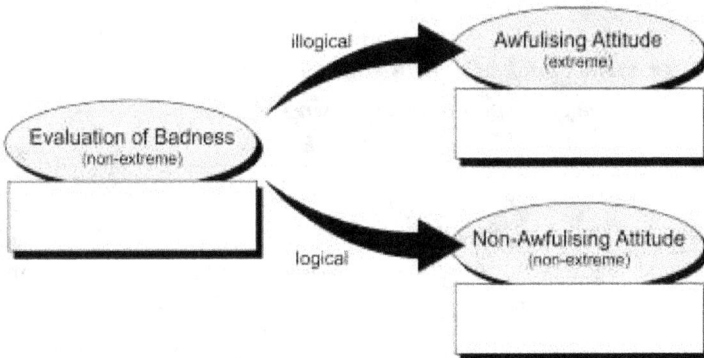

Figure 2: An awfulising attitude is illogical, while a non-awfulising attitude is logical

Your coachee's non-awfulising attitude is as follows:

> *It would be very bad if X happened (or did not happen) …*
> *but it would not be terrible.*

Encourage your coachee to see that their non-awfulising attitude is logical since both parts are non-extreme and thus the second component logically follows from the first. Again, use the template in Figure 2 with your coachee to illustrate this point visually, if necessary.

13.3   The pragmatic question

Ask:

Which of the following attitudes leads to largely good results and which leads to largely poor results and why?

- *The coachee's awfulising attitude*
- *The coachee's non-awfulising attitude*

You need to help your coachee acknowledge that their awfulising attitude leads to largely unconstructive results, while their non-awfulising attitude leads to more constructive ones. As you do this, use the information provided by your coachee when you discussed the two *B–C* connections (see Step 10).

If your coachee thinks their awfulising attitude leads to healthier consequences than their flexible attitude, help them through discussion to see why they are likely to be mistaken.

13.4   Assess the coachee's commitment to attitude change

At this point, you want to assess your coachee's commitment to change their attitude. You do this by asking the following question:

Ask:

Which attitude does the coachee want to strengthen, and which do they want to weaken and why?

- *The coachee's awfulising attitude*
- *The coachee's non-awfulising attitude*

After helping your coachee to examine their awfulising and non-awfulising attitudes, your coachee 'should' indicate that they wish to work to strengthen their conviction in their non-awfulising attitude and weaken their conviction in their awfulising attitude and be able to give coherent reasons why based on their problematic feelings and behaviour and their goals for change. If your coachee gives you any other answer, discover the reasons for this response and work with them until they fully commit to their non-awfulising attitude.

Step 14

Help the Coachee to Examine an Unbearability Attitude and Its Bearability Attitude Alternative

Unbearability Attitude	Bearability Attitude
• *It would be a struggle for me to bear it if X happens (or does not happen, and therefore I could not bear it*	• *It would be a struggle for me to bear it if X happens (or does not happen), but I could bear it. It would be worth it to me to do so, and I am worth bearing it for. I am willing to bear it, and I am going to bear it.*

When helping your coachee examine their unbearability and bearability attitudes, use the same three questions you used to help them examine their rigid and flexible attitudes: the empirical, logical, and pragmatic. Once you have done this, you can ask which attitude your coachee wants to strengthen, which they want to weaken, and why.

54

As before, begin by suggesting that your coachee focus on their unbearability attitude and their bearability attitude alternative. Encourage them to write both attitudes down side by side (as above)[9] or write them down yourself on a whiteboard (again, as above). Then, move on to the three questions.

14.1 The empirical question

Ask:

Which of the following attitudes is true and which is false and why?

- *The coachee's unbearability attitude*
- *The coachee's bearability attitude*

According to REBT theory, an unbearability attitude is false, and a bearability attitude is true.

While examining these attitudes, help your coachee see that when they are holding their unbearability attitude, they believe the following:

- I will die or disintegrate if the adversity continues to exist
- I will lose the capacity to experience happiness if the adversity continues to exist.

---

[9] Yet again, you will be working with their specific unbearability and bearability attitudes.

Help your coachee to see that both these convictions are inconsistent with reality and that their unbearability attitude is false. By contrast, help them to see that their bearability attitude is true since this is made up of the following ideas:

- I will struggle if the adversity continues to exist, but I will neither die nor disintegrate;
- I will not lose the capacity to experience happiness if the adversity continues to exist, although this capacity will be temporarily diminished; and
- The adversity worth bearing.
- I am worth bearing the adversity for
- I am willing to bear it
- I am going to bear it

If your coachee gives you an answer that is at variance with the above, then help them through discussion to see why their answer is incorrect and help them to accept the correct answer.

14.2   The logical question

Ask:

Which of the following attitudes is logical and which is illogical, and why?

- *The coachee's unbearability attitude*
- *The coachee's bearability attitude*

Your coachee needs to acknowledge that their unbearability attitude is illogical while their bearability attitude is logical. Help them to see that unbearability attitude is based on the same struggle component as their bearability flexible attitude, but that they transform it as follows:

> *It would be a struggle for me to bear it if X happened (or did not happen .... and therefore it would be unbearable*

Show the coachee that this attitude has two components. The first [It would be a struggle for me to bear it if X happened (or did not happen)] is not extreme, but the second [...and therefore it would be unbearable] is extreme. As such, the coachee's unbearability attitude isn't logical since one cannot logically derive something extreme from something that is not extreme rigid. Use the template in Figure 3 with your coachee to illustrate this point visually, if necessary.

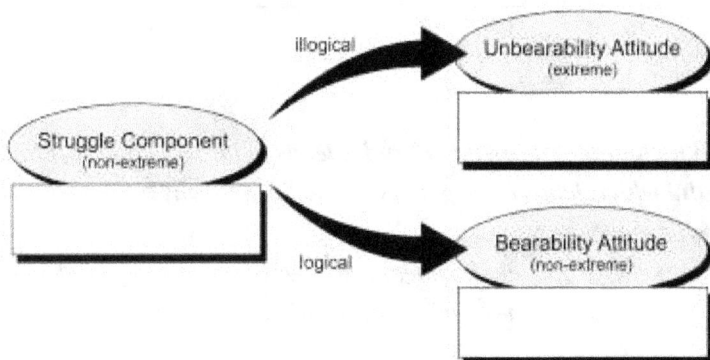

Figure 3: An unbearability attitude is illogical, while a bearability attitude is logical

Your coachee's bearability attitude is as follows:

> • *It would be a struggle for me to bear it if X happens (or does not happen), but I could bear it. It would be worth it to me to do so, and I am worth bearing it for. I am willing to bear it, and I am going to bear it.*

The coachee's bearability attitude is logical since all of its components are not extreme and are thus logically connected due to their non-extreme nature. Again, use the template in Figure 3 with your coachee to illustrate this visually, if necessary.

If your coachee gives you any other answer, then help them through discussion to see why their answer is incorrect and help them to accept the correct answer.

14.3   The pragmatic question

> Ask:
>
> *Which of the following attitudes leads to largely good results and which leads to largely poor results and why?*
>
> • *The coachee's unbearability attitude*
> • *The coachee's bearability attitude*

You need to help your coachee acknowledge that their unbearability attitude leads to largely unconstructive results, while their bearability attitude leads to more constructive ones.

As you do this, use the information provided by your coachee when you discussed the two B–C connections (see Step 10).

If your coachee thinks their unbearability attitude leads to healthier consequences than their bearability attitude, help them through discussion to see why they are likely to be mistaken.

14.4 Assess the coachee's commitment to attitude change

At this point, you want to assess your coachee's commitment to change their attitude. You do this by asking the following question:

Ask:

Which attitude do you want to strengthen, and which do you want to weaken and why?

After helping your coachee to examine their unbearability and bearability attitudes, your coachee 'should' indicate that they wish to work to strengthen their conviction in their bearability attitude and weaken their conviction in their unbearability attitude and be able to give coherent reasons why based on their problematic feelings and behaviour and their goals for change. If your coachee gives you any other answer, discover the reasons for this response and work with them until they fully commit to their bearability attitude.

STEP 15

Help the Coachee to Examine a Devaluation Attitude and Its Unconditional Acceptance Attitude Alternative

Devaluation Attitude	Unconditional Acceptance Attitude
• *If X happens (or does not happen), it proves that:* - *I am no good or* - *You are no good or* - *Life is no good*	• *If X happens (or does not happen), it does not prove that:* - *I am no good or* - *You are no good or* - *Life is no good* *It proves that:* - *I am a complex, unrateable fallible human being* - *You are a complex, unrateable human being* - *Life is a complex mixture of good, bad and neutral and is thus unrateable*

When helping your coachee examine their devaluation and unconditional acceptance attitudes, again use the same three questions you used to help them examine their rigid and flexible attitudes: empirical, logical, and pragmatic. Once you have done this, you can ask which attitude your coachee wants to strengthen, which they want to weaken, and why.

Once again, begin by suggesting that your coachee focus on their devaluation attitude and their unconditional acceptance attitude alternative. As before, encourage your coachee to write both attitudes side by side (as above)[10] or write them down yourself on a whiteboard (again, as above). Then move on to the three questions.

15.1 The empirical question

Ask:

Which of the following attitudes is true and which is false and why?

- *The coachee's devaluation attitude*
- *The coachee's unconditional acceptance attitude*

According to REBT theory, an unconditional acceptance attitude is true, and a devaluation attitude is false.

---

[10] As before, you will be working with their specific devaluation and unconditional acceptance attitudes.

15.1.1 Helping your coachee to examine the empirical status of their person-devaluation (self- or other-) attitude and its unconditional acceptance attitude alternative

Help your coachee to see that when they hold a person-devaluation attitude towards themself or another person, they believe the following:

- A person (self or other) can legitimately be given a single global rating that defines their essence and the worth of a person is dependent upon conditions that change (e.g. my worth goes up when I do well and goes down when I don't do well)
- A person can be rated based on one of their aspects

Help your coachee to see that these convictions are inconsistent with reality and that their person-devaluation attitude is false. By contrast, help them to see that their unconditional acceptance attitude held towards themself or another person is true since this is made up of the following ideas:

- A person cannot legitimately be given a single global rating that defines their essence and their worth, as far as they have it, is not dependent upon conditions that change (e.g. my worth stays the same whether or not I do well)
- It makes sense to rate discrete aspects of a person, but it does not make sense to rate a person based on these discrete aspects since the person is far too complex to merit such a rating

15.1.2 Helping your coachee to examine the empirical status of their life-devaluation attitude and its unconditional acceptance attitude alternative

Help your coachee see that when they hold a life-devaluation attitude, they believe the following:

- The world can legitimately be given a single rating that defines its essential nature and that the value of the world varies according to what happens within it (e.g. the value of the world goes up when something fair occurs and goes down when something unfair happens)
- The world can be rated based on one of its aspects.

Help your coachee see that these convictions are inconsistent with reality and that their life-devaluation attitude is false. By contrast, help them to see that their unconditional life-acceptance attitude is true since this is made up of the following ideas:

- Life cannot legitimately be given a single rating that defines its essential nature, and its value does not vary according to what happens within it (e.g. the value of life stays the same whether fairness exists at any given time or not)
- It makes sense to rate discrete aspects of life, but it does not make sense to rate life based on these discrete aspects since life is far to complex to merit such a rating

If your coachee gives you an answer that is at variance with the above, then help them through discussion to see why their response is incorrect and help them accept the correct answer.

15.2   The logical question

Ask:

Which of the following attitudes is logical and which is logical and why?

- *The coachee's devaluation attitude*
- *The coachee's unconditional acceptance attitude*

Help your coachee see that their devaluation attitude is illogical, while their unconditional acceptance attitude is logical[11].

For example, if your coachee holds a self-devaluation attitude show them that this attitude is based on the same idea as their unconditional self-acceptance attitude in that in both they acknowledge that it is bad if X happened, for example, but that they transform it as follows:

---

[11] The points in this section also apply to a coachee's life-devaluation and unconditional life-acceptance attitudes.

X is bad... and therefore I am bad

For example:

It would be bad if my line manager criticises my work and if he does it proves I am worthless.

Here, the coachee's self-devaluation attitude has two components. The first (X is bad...) is the coachee's evaluation of a part of their experience, while the second (...and therefore I am bad) is their evaluation of the whole of their *self*. As such, the coachee is making the illogical part–whole error where the part is deemed illogically to define the whole.

Your coachee's unconditional self-acceptance attitude is as follows:

X is bad, but this does not mean that I am bad. I am a fallible human being even though X happened

For example:

It would be bad if my line manager criticises my work. If he does, it does not prove I am worthless. I am the same unrateable, complex fallible human being whether he criticises my work or not.

Encourage your coachee to see that their unconditional self-acceptance attitude is logical because it shows that their *self* is complex and incorporates a bad event. Thus, in holding their unconditional self-acceptance attitude, the coachee avoids making the part–whole error.

15.3   The pragmatic question

Ask:

Which of the following attitudes leads to largely good results and which leads to largely poor results and why?

- *The coachee's devaluation attitude*
- *The coachee's unconditional acceptance attitude*

You need to help your coachee acknowledge that their devaluation attitude leads to largely unconstructive results, while their unconditional acceptance attitude leads to more constructive ones. As you do this, use the information provided by your coachee when you discussed the two *B–C* connections (see Step 10).

If your coachee thinks their devaluation attitude leads to healthier consequences than their unconditional acceptance attitude, help them through discussion to see why they are likely to be mistaken.

15.4 Assess the coachee's commitment to attitude change

At this point, you want to assess your coachee's commitment to change their attitude. You do this by asking the following question:

Ask:

Which attitude do you want to strengthen, and which do you want to weaken and why?

After helping your coachee to examine their devaluation and unconditional acceptance attitudes, your coachee 'should' indicate that they wish to work to strengthen their conviction in their unconditional acceptance attitude and weaken their conviction in their devaluation attitude and be able to give coherent reasons why based on their problematic feelings and behaviour and their goals for change. If your coachee gives you any other answer, discover the reasons for this response and work with them until they fully commit to their unconditional acceptance attitude.

STEP 16

Help the Coachee to Strengthen Their Conviction in Their Flexible/Non-Extreme Attitudes and Weaken Their Conviction in Their Rigid/Extreme Attitudes

There are two types of insight in REBT: intellectual and emotional insight. When your coachee has intellectual insight, they understand why their rigid/extreme attitudes are false, illogical and unhelpful and their flexible/non-extreme attitudes are true. logical and helpful, but this insight has little impact on their feelings and behaviour. However, when they have emotional insight, this understanding has great impact on their feelings and behaviour. When they have intellectual insight into their rigid/extreme attitudes and flexible/non-extreme attitudes, they can 'talk the talk', but when they have emotional insight, she can 'walk the talk'! Explain to them what they need to do to move from intellectual insight to emotional insight.

16.1 Explain the process of change

Explain to your coachee that while they may have preferred something to happen (or not happen), it doesn't have to happen (or not happen) and if they understand what you say but don't believe it, encourage them to see that they need to practise the new attitude and act on it ('walk the talk') while tolerating the discomfort of doing so, and as they do it their conviction in it will grow.

16.2 Techniques to help your coachee gain conviction in their flexible/non-extreme attitudes

In this section, I will describe three techniques to help your coachee to develop their conviction in the flexible/non-extreme attitudes.

16.2.1 Attack-response (or zig-zag) technique. Your coachee can strengthen their conviction in a flexible/non-extreme attitude by responding persuasively to attacks on it (see Dryden, 2022).

16.2.1.1 *Instructions to your coachee in completing a written attack-response form*

- Write down your specific flexible/non-extreme attitude and present level of conviction in it on a 100% point scale (0% = no conviction, 100% = total conviction).
- Write down an attack on this in the form of a doubt, reservation or objection; include an explicit rigid/extreme attitude (e.g. rigid attitude, awfulising attitude, unbearability attitude or devaluation attitude). Make this attack as genuine as possible: the more it reflects your attitudes.
- Respond to each element of this attack as fully as possible, including rigid/extreme attitude statements and distorted or unrealistic inferences framed in the form of a doubt, reservation or objection to the flexible/non-extreme attitude.

Do so as persuasively as possible and write down your response.

- Continue until you have answered all your attacks and can't think of any more. Keep your focus on the flexible/non-extreme attitude you are committed to strengthen. If you find this difficult, make your attacks gently at first. When you can respond to these attacks easily, make them more biting. Work in this way until you're making really strong attacks. Make them as if you really want to believe them. When you respond, throw yourself into it to demolish the attack. The purpose of this exercise is to strengthen conviction in your flexible/non-extreme attitude, so it is important that you stop only when you have answered all your attacks. If you make an attack you can't respond to, stop the exercise and raise the matter with me in your next session.

- When you have answered all your attacks, re-rate your level of conviction in your flexible/non-extreme attitude using the 0–100% scale. If you succeed in responding persuasively to your attacks, this rating will go up appreciably.

If your coachee's conviction level in their flexible/non-extreme attitude has not increased or only increases a little, discuss this with them so you can both discover what is preventing an increase in their level of conviction.

16.2.2 Rational-emotive imagery (REI)

This imagery method is designed to help your coachee practice changing their *specific* rigid/extreme attitude at B to its flexible/non-extreme equivalent while imagining what they are most disturbed about in the specific *Situation* in question. Help them understand that this method will strengthen their conviction in their new flexible/non-extreme attitudes.

16.2.2.1   Instructions for using REI

- Take a *Situation* in which you disturbed yourself, identifying which aspect you were most disturbed about.

- Close your eyes, imagine the *Situation* as vividly as possible, focusing on the adversity at *A*.

- Allow yourself to experience fully the UNE you felt at the time while still focusing intently on the *A*. Ensure the UNE is one of the following: anxiety, depression, shame, guilt, hurt, unhealthy regret, unhealthy anger, unhealthy jealousy, unhealthy envy.

- Really experience this disturbed emotion for a moment or two; then change your emotional response to an HNE, while focusing intently on the adversity at *A*. Don't change the intensity of the emotion, just the emotion itself. If your original UNE was anxiety, change it to concern. Change depression to sadness; shame to disappointment; guilt to remorse; hurt to sorrow; unhealthy regret to healthy regret, unhealthy anger to healthy anger; unhealthy jealousy to healthy jealousy; unhealthy envy to healthy envy. Change the UNE to its healthy equivalent but keep the level of intensity of the new emotion as strong as the old emotion. Keep experiencing this new emotion for about five minutes, while focusing on the adversity at *A*. If you go back to the old UNE, bring back the new HNE.

After five minutes, ask your coachee how they changed their emotion. Ensure they changed their emotional response by changing their specific rigid/extreme attitude to its flexible/non-extreme attitude alternative. If they didn't (e.g. if they changed their emotion by changing the *A* to make it less negative or neutral or by holding an indifference attitude towards the *A*), suggest they do the exercise again. Keep doing this until they have changed their emotion only by changing their specific rigid/extreme attitude to its flexible/non-extreme attitude alternative. Encourage them to practise REI several times a day and to aim for 30 minutes' daily practice when they are not doing any other therapy homework.

16.2.3 Suggest that your coachee rehearse their flexible/non-extreme attitude while acting in ways consistent with this attitude

Perhaps the most powerful way of helping your coachee to strengthen their conviction in their flexible/non-extreme attitude is to encourage them to rehearse it while facing the relevant adversity at A and acting in ways consistent with this attitude.

End a coaching session by negotiating a homework assignment that helps your coachee implement the above principle, based on the work you have already done in the session. Remember the following equation when negotiating a behavioural homework assignment:

Face adversity at A + rehearse the flexible/non-extreme attitude + act in ways consistent with this attitude

---

STEP 17

Negotiate Homework Assignments

While homework assignments are traditionally negotiated at the end of coaching sessions, they can be agreed earlier. Ensure the coachee understands what They are going to do at the end of the session.

17.1 Principles in negotiating assignments

The following are a number of principles to keep in mind in mind while negotiating a homework assignment with your coachee.

17.1.1 Use a term for assignments acceptable to your coachee

While the generic term for a task your coachee carries out between sessions is homework assignment, some coachees respond negatively to the term since it reminds them of school with its negative connotations. If so, use a more acceptable term.

17.1.2 Negotiate assignments with your coachee. Do not assign them unilaterally

Coaching is based on a collaborative relationship between coach and coachee, reflected in your stance towards assignments. Negotiate assignments with them rather than assigning them unilaterally.

17.1.3 Allow time in the session to negotiate assignments

Time is at a premium in coaching sessions. You have much to do in helping your coachee address their emotional problem effectively. You may reach the end of the session and realise you haven't negotiated a relevant assignment with them. To avoid this, prioritise negotiating assignments in your mind and use a visible prompt as a reminder during the session. Allocating the last ten minutes to such negotiation is a good rule of thumb.

17.1.4 Ensure assignments follow logically from session work

The assignment should provide a logical bridge between session work and what your coachee has agreed to do between sessions.

17.1.5 Ensure your coachee clearly understands the assignment

If they do not understand what they have agreed to do, they are unlikely to do it.

17.1.6 Ensure assignments are relevant to your coachee's dealing effectively with their emotional problem

If your coachee doesn't understand how the assignment will help them achieve their emotional goals and deal effectively with their emotional problem, they will again be unlikely to do the task.

17.1.7 Ensure the type of assignment you negotiate with your coachee is relevant to the stage reached by both of you on their emotional problem

There are several types of assignments and it's important that what your coachee agrees to do is relevant to where you have got to in dealing with their emotional problem. Thus, reading assignments are best suited to helping them understand more about their emotional problem; cognitive assignments are best in giving them practice at examining their attitudes and cognitive-behavioural assignments are best for helping them act on their flexible/non-extreme attitude while simultaneously rehearsing it.

17.1.8 Employ the *challenging but not overwhelming* principle in negotiating assignments

If you ask your coachee to do something that is beyond them, they won't do it. If you ask them to do something too easy, they will gain little therapeutic value from the task. However, if you suggest they do something they can do, but which will be difficult for them, they are likely to do it and gain from doing so.

17.1.9 Introduce and explain the *no-lose* concept of assignments

The *no-lose* concept points to the fact that when your coachee does an assignment successfully they gain from doing so, but if they fail, it provides an opportunity to learn more about obstacles to change so you can both effectively address such obstacles. The latter should be stressed when your coachee feels discouraged in failing to do an assignment.

17.1.10   Ensure your coachee has the skills to undertake the assignment

If your coachee dos not have the required skills to do their homework, it is unlikely they will do this or they will do it poorly. If so, teach them these skills before suggesting they implement the assignment.

17.1.11   Ensure your coachee thinks they can do the assignment

Your coachee may have the skills to do the assignment but may think they can't do it. Encourage them to use imagery rehearsal in the session, where they picture themself successfully completing the assignment, and to practise this technique between sessions before doing the task in actuality. Such imagery rehearsal may help them see that they can do what they previously thought they couldn't do.

17.1.12   Elicit a firm commitment to carry out the assignment

It is sometimes useful for your coachee to make a commitment to do an assignment. This may be with themself, with you or with a friend. If doing so increases the chances that she will carry out the assignment, it is a useful technique.

17.1.13   Help your coachee specify when, where and how often they will carry out the assignment

Hitherto, I have stressed the value of being specific as you assess your coachee's emotional problem and intervene accordingly. This principle is also useful in homework negotiation and, if the assignment warrants it, encourage your coachee to specify when, where and how often they will do the task. In my experience, encouraging coachees to be specific reduces the chances that they will say that they didn't do the assignment because they didn't have time or opportunity to do so.

17.1.14 Help your coachee rehearse the assignment during the session

If you have time, encouraging your coachee to rehearse the assignment in the session can be valuable. Rehearsal may be mental (they picture themself carrying out the assignment in their mind's eye) or behavioural (they role-play with you what they have agreed to do when that involves another person). In the latter case, you may need to know a little about the other person if you are to play their role plausibly. Encourage your coachee to practice their flexible/non-extreme attitude before and during the rehearsal.

17.1.15 Elicit from the coachee potential obstacles to homework completion and problem-solve these obstacles

The more you encourage your coachee to identify potential obstacles to doing a negotiated assignment and either help them circumvent such obstacles or neutralise them, the more they are likely to do the assignment. Unidentified obstacles will prevent them from carrying out their assignment.

17.1.16 Encourage your coachee to make and retain a written note of the assignment and its relevant details

Medical studies show that when a patient is given a written note by the physician of what medication to take, when and how often, this increases patient compliance with the medication. This is useful in coaching too: encourage your coachee to make a written note of the assignment and related issues (e.g. time, place and frequency). Make a written note of this in your notes. Check that you both have an accurate record of the negotiated assignment if you suspect this may not be the case.

STEP 18

Review Homework Assignments

Negotiating suitable assignments shows your coachee that they are an integral part of dealing with their emotional problem. However, you can undermine this if you fail to review them]se assignments at the beginning of the following session. Unless there is a very good reason not to (e.g. your coachee is in a state of crisis), it is good coaching practice to review the assignment at the outset of the next session and devote sufficient time to the review to underscore its importance.

18.1   Principles in reviewing assignments with your coachee

The following are a number of principles to keep in mind in mind while reviewing a homework assignment with your coachee

18.1.1   Check whether the assignment was done as negotiated

When your coachee reports that they carried out the assignment, check when you review the assignment whether they did it as negotiated. They may have changed the nature of the assignment and thus lessened its therapeutic potency. For example, they may not have faced the critical aspect of the *Situation* they had agreed to face (in REBT parlance, they did not face the *A*).

Suppose your coachee has a fear of being rejected by a particular man. You negotiated an assignment with her whereby she agreed to ask a man for a date. She reports that she is pleased with the result of the assignment. She asked a man if he wanted to go for coffee with her and he accepts her invitation. However, you know that the *A* she agreed to face was asking the man for a date. As the two are colleagues they often go for coffee and the man wouldn't have seen your coachee's invitation as a 'date'. From a therapeutic point of view she hasn't faced the 'A' she agreed to face, i.e. the prospect of a date. She played safe.

18.1.2 How to respond when your coachee has changed the nature of their homework.

Here is how I suggest you respond when your coachee has changed the nature of their agreed homework assignment:

- Encourage them by saying you were pleased they did the assignment.
- Explain how, in your opinion, the coachee changed the assignment. Remind them of the exact nature of the task as negotiated by the two of you in the previous session. In doing so, if indicated, remind them of the purpose of the assignment which dictated its precise form.
- If your coachee made a genuine mistake in changing the nature of the assignment, invite them to redo it, but as previously negotiated. If they agrees, ensure they keep a written reminder of the assignment and ask them to guard against making further changes to it. Review the assignment in the following session. If your coachee does not agree to do the assignment, explore and deal with their reluctance.

- If the change your coachee made to the assignment appears to be motivated by the presence of an implicit rigid/extreme attitude, identify and deal with this attitude. Then, invite them to redo the assignment as previously negotiated, urging them again to guard against making further changes to the assignment. Alternatively, modify the assignment in a way that takes into account the newly discovered obstacle.

18.1.3 Review what your coachee learned from the assignment

Ask your coachee what they learned from the assignment. If they learned what you hoped they would learn, acknowledge that they did well and move on. If they didn't learn from the assignment, you should address this issue. Help them learn the appropriate point and to choose another assignment that will help them put this point into practice so their learning is experiential, not just cognitive.

18.1.4 Capitalise on your coachee's success

When your coachee has successfully done their homework and learned what you hoped they would learn, reinforce their achievement, suggesting they build on their success by choosing a more challenging assignment next time, if appropriate.

18.1.5 Responding to your coachee's homework *failure*

When coachees have done their homework but it turned out poorly, they often say they did the assignment, but *it didn't work.* *Failure* is italicised here because there's much to learn from this *Situation.* When you encounter so-called *failure,* remind your coachee of the 'no-lose' nature of homework assignments and investigate the factors involved. Ask for a factual account of what happened. Once you have identified the factors accounting for the *failure*, help your coachee deal with them and then renegotiate the same or a similar assignment. Here is an illustrative list of common reasons for homework *failure* and possible therapeutic responses.

18.1.5.1 Problem: Your coachee implemented certain, but not all elements of the assignment, e.g. they did the behavioural part of the assignment, but did not practise their new flexible/non-extreme attitude. They therefore experienced the same UNE associated with their nominated problem.

Response: Suggest they remember to rehearse their flexible/non-extreme attitude before the behavioural part of the task. Use an in-session imagery technique if required.

18.1.5.2 Problem: The assignment was 'overwhelming, rather than challenging' for them at this time.

Response: Encourage them to see this as good feedback; recalibrate the assignment so it is 'challenging' rather than 'overwhelming'.

18.1.5.3 Problem: Your coachee began to do the assignment but stopped after experiencing discomfort which they believed they couldn't bear.

Response: Help them formulate an appropriate bearability attitude; suggest that they rehearse this the next time it happens.

18.1.5.4 Problem: Your coachee practised the wrong flexible/non-extreme attitude during the assignment.

Response: Ascertain the reason for this; suggest a suitable remedy. Suggest that they write the correct attitude on a card and take it with them to review in relevant *Situations*.

18.1.5.5 Problem: Your coachee practised the right flexible/non-extreme attitude, but did it weakly so their UNE predominated.

Response: Suggest that they be more forceful with themself in rehearsing their flexible/non-extreme attitude. Model this in the session if necessary.

18.1.5.6 Problem: Your coachee began the assignment but forgot what they were to do.

Response: Suggest that they consult a written record of the assignment. If they 'forget' to do so, the obstacle needs further assessment.

18.1.5.7 Problem: Your coachee began the assignment but gave up because they didn't experience immediate benefit from it.

Response: Help them see that while immediate benefit would be nice, it isn't necessary or likely. Help them take a longer-range view of such benefit.

18.1.5.8 Problem: Your coachee began the assignment but gave up soon after when they realised they didn't know what to do. This happens particularly with written *ABC* assignments.

Response: Give them a set of written instructions (see Dryden, 2022, for examples).

18.1.5.9   Problem: Your coachee began the assignment but encountered another *A* which triggered a new undiscovered rigid/extreme attitude which led them to abandon the assignment.

Response: Suggest that if this happens again, they look for and examine and change the new rigid/extreme attitude before returning to the agreed task.

18.1.6 Dealing with the *Situation* if your coachee hasn't done the assignment

Although you may have taken care in negotiating an assignment, instituting all safeguards discussed above, your coachee may still not carry it out. If so, ask them for a factual account of the *Situation* where she contracted to do the assignment but didn't do it, reminding them of the 'no-lose' concept of assignments; identify and deal with factors accounting for them not doing the assignment and then renegotiate the same or similar assignment. As you investigate these factors, be aware that you may have failed to institute one or more safeguards reviewed above. If so, and your failure accounts for your coachee not carrying out the assignment, take responsibility for this omission, disclose this to them, institute the safeguard and renegotiate the assignment. However, if the reason why your coachee didn't do the assignment can be attributed to a factor internal to them that you couldn't have foreseen, help them deal with it and again renegotiate the same or similar assignment.

STEP 19

Revisit and Examine *A* if Necessary

After you have helped your coachee along the pathway to attitude change, at a suitable point, it is useful to examine *A* with them, particularly if it is clear that *A* is/was negatively distorted.

19.1   How to question *A*

Help your coachee examine *A* by returning to it and asking whether this was the most realistic way of looking at the *Situation*. This doesn't mean they can know for certain that their *A* was true or false, for there is rarely any absolute, agreed way of viewing an event. What it does mean is that your coachee can weigh up all the evidence available to them about the *Situation* and make the *best bet* about what happened.

19.1.1   Encourage your coachee to go back to their *ABC*, focusing on what they wrote under the heading *Situation*

Then, ask them whether what they listed under *A* was the most realistic way of viewing the *Situation* given all the evidence. This involves your coachee considering the inference they made that formed *A*, considering alternative inferences, evaluating all possibilities and choosing the most realistic inference.

19.1.2 Other questions you can ask your coachee about *A*

- How likely is it that *A* happened (or might happen)?
- Would an objective jury agree that *A* happened or might happen? If not, what would the jury's verdict be?
- Did you view (are you viewing) the *Situation* realistically? If not, how could you have viewed (can you view) it more realistically?
- If you asked someone whom you could trust to give you an objective opinion about the truth or falsity of your inference about the *Situation* at hand, what would they say to you and why? How would they encourage you to view the *Situation* instead.
- If a friend told you they had faced (were facing or were about to face) the same *Situation* as you faced and made the same inference, what would you say to them about the validity of their inference and why? How would you encourage them to view the *Situation* instead?

We have now reached the end of the book. I hope that you have found it useful. If you have any feedback for me about the book, I would be pleased to receive it at: windy@windydryden.com

References

Dryden, W. (2017). *The Coaching Alliance: Theory and Guidelines for Practice*. Routledge.

Dryden, W. (2022). *Reason to Change: A Rational Emotive Behaviour Therapy (REBT) Workbook. 2nd Edition*. Routledge.

Index

89

www.ingramcontent.com/pod-product-compliance
Lightning Source LLC
Chambersburg PA
CBHW050550280326
41933CB00011B/1787